Bare Ruined Choirs

Tom Kepler

"Bare ruined choirs where late the sweet birds sang."

William Shakespeare
Sonnet 73

Wise Moon Books
2130 Emerald Lane
Fairfield, IA 52556

http://www.tomkeplerswritingblog.com
http://sites.google.com/site/tomkeplerwriting

Bare Ruined Choirs
Tom Kepler

© Thomas L. Kepler 2009

ISBN 978-0-9842734-0-9

All rights reserved. Except for brief passages quoted in a newspaper, magazine, radio, television, or online review, no part of this book may be reproduced without the written permission of Wise Moon Books.

Dedicated to
Barbara Jean Kepler
(1946-2003)
mother and wife

and

Nevin Brian Kepler
son extraordinaire

Acknowledgements

"Sleeping Magnolia"	*California Quarterly*	1974
"Saturday Morning"	*Riverrun*	1988
"Silence Heard Twice"	*Wind*	1992
"My Son Sleeping," "Winter Solstice"	*The Hiram Poetry Review*	1993
"Burning Arguments to the Contrary"	*The Galley Sail Review*	1994
"Afternoon Adventure, Jefferson County Park" "Mother Rose" (originally published as "Aunt Rose") "Following My Son's Footsteps," "The Winters"	*The Iowa Source*	1994
"Words for My Son," from the anthology *Leaves by Night, Flowers by Day*, 1st World Publishing		2006

My deepest appreciation and love to Sandy, who lets me follow my path. I am still awed by the miracle that transformed the angel next door into my loving wife.

To Allen Cobb, thank you for patiently teaching me what I need to know to take a manuscript and turn it into a book.

To Lucinda Hall, for befriending me in my digital hour of need.

To Ronald Allen Loch, master teacher, to fulfill a very old promise.

Contents

Sleeping Magnolia 1
Island 2
Saturday Morning 3
Honeydew 4
Silence Heard Twice 5
The Flower 6
My Son Sleeping 7
Following My Son's Footsteps 8
Afternoon Adventure, Jefferson County Park 9
November Night 10
Words for My Son 11
Burning Arguments to the Contrary 12
Hydrangeas in November 13
A Blues Note 14
The Winters 15
Resurrection 16
Reflection 17
Three Skies 18
Adoration of Asters 19
Affirmations at the Mouth of the Well 20
Bare Ruined Choirs 22
For the Life of Me 23
Cave Swallow 24
I Forgive Your Death 25
Mother Rose 26
Into the Light 27
Winter Solstice 28
Winter Pasture 29

Sonnet 73, by William Shakespeare 31
A Note on the Title 32

About the Author 33

Book It Forward: a Letter to the Reader 35

Sleeping Magnolia

Whose tight flowers
are drops of opaque oil
cupped by black
waxy leaves?

Whose spiderweb fragrance
captures the night
in a net
of loose wind?

Whose root fingernails
scratching
the black skin of earth
redden dusk and dawn?

A magnolia woman sleeps
beneath a wax leaf tree:
opaque necklace of her breasts,
ruffled sheets of wind,
black earth beneath long fingernails.

Island

This is what I see...

a wide stretch of river,
cottonwoods
peering lazily into water

oars slip-slipping,
eddies of baywood and crayfish,
rowboat sliding upstream

and one green feather of island
slurring water,
succulent seed of sun-moist loam.

Saturday Morning

Rain trembles in the leaves
its luscious, liquid staccato,
spatters the dawn-warmed asphalt,

strikes metallic melodies
from the wire strands
of the window screen.

Moist in the music of silence,
I sit upstairs on my bed
beside the lichen-greened hackberry tree

outside the open window—
immersed this Saturday morning
in meaningless, inconsequential glories.

Honeydew

When I change your breasts to honeydew,
then my mouth waters for your flesh,
warm and pale as you lie in bed,

a tangle of shadow and afternoon light.
The weight of your breasts pulls my hands
to touch this fruit, warm and moist.

During these dog days of summer,
heat greens you, my wife, my melon.
Like lettuce planted late, I bolt early,

am spent, my honeydew, before you freckle
with sugar, heavy on the vine.
By root and thistle, by weed and damselfly,

by sweat which rimes your nipples,
a pollen-drunk bee in the melon patch,
I fly the flowers of your august thighs.

Silence Heard Twice

You say that the hermit in me enjoys
being left to these times of solitude,
to these times of echoes,

to be stripped clean of sound and abandoned.
This afternoon I abandoned myself
to truths to be traced

in the hardwood. Light fell in patterned,
lambent beams on the tongue-and-groove oak floor.
Where the fiber of light

and wood merged, I placed my hands to the warmth,
to the warm-grained clarity of silence,
to the coming and going

of my living, to my heartbeat's heartwood
and its glad echo of inspiration.
And now I say

silence is always heard twice: silence mute
with memory at your leaving; memories rich
in silence at your return.

The Flower

Bell-shaped blossoms cluster
next to limbs of the catalpa tree,
garland sky above the sidewalk.

Arched branches of silent chiming,
ivory petals shade my son sleeping,
face as flawless as any flower.

My Son Sleeping

I ease beneath the covers
to share his silent sleeping.

Perhaps I dream my son sleeping,
glowing like an ember
        or an infant star,

breathing warmth into the night.
The audacity of our hearts beating
        in this cold space!

Reaching out in his dreaming,
my son slides his small hand
        along the cotton sheet,

confirms the constellation
of my breathing as gently
        as his mother's touch.

There is no lonely cold
within the orbit of his breathing.
        The least touch suffices,

lights his sleeping half-smile.
That I am not alone and dreaming
        darkness from the void—

that I am with my son sleeping
is sufficient light for me.

Following My Son's Footsteps

The shovel rusts, wet with rain again,
and the red Radio Flyer puddles reflections
while frost-scorched chives push green through mulch.
My son's map is drawn as it happens—
a blaze of scuffs, his own haphazard direction.
He shovels sand to wagon; then it's push

or pull or leave it lay and find something else—
trucks daffodil yellow or box elder orange,
the untilled garden stirred to a sticky mud.
Guided by grapevines, trailing sun till it leans,
I angle along crystals within geodes, gaze at strange
eggs, follow footprints past slender branches, swollen bud.

Past crows and caws, swales and sunlit cloud,
I green in seas my son has sailed, root in earth he's plowed.

Afternoon Adventure, Jefferson County Park

You wanted orioles flitting among shagbark hickories,
box turtles dimpling green-tinted pond water.
Oriole, turtle, pond and sky,
we'd make a game of the giving of names.

You wanted a swinging bridge
cabled above a fern-lush ravine,
an owl sleeping among juniper berries,
pebbles tiling creek bottom, twigs close to hand.

You wanted a father pleased with your leaps,
eager to follow the rain-soft slope of your tracks,
to school you in minnows warm in shallows,
to find the highwater mark, its driftwood mosaic.

I am your father, pleased with your leaps,
attempting bravery beneath green leaves:
to back off and pretend not to catch your fall,
to keep you brave, yet keep you in the game.

November Night

Tonight I turn in early,
warm in the shell of my blankets.
Light pearls the window.

Mother and son murmur drowsy currents,
voices settling like waves
lulled back to ocean.

The sandy season of crickets is past.
Rain is misting the bedroom window.
In three days the first snow will fall.

I can imagine no life more exciting.

Words for My Son

Words, like wood, will warm the evening air.
We settle, coals within our bed,
blanketed thigh by thigh,
light ruddy with our words.

Your hand rises like woodsmoke into my hair.
Words twine and twist, shadows gather,
and in the shadows, spiders weave their patient webs.

Listen to the words as they crackle and pop,
whole pages flaring, flames thumbing
rough-barked logs, stars craning overhead,

reading over our shoulders words illuminated,
banked with marrow of meaning enough
to warm us through the long, cold night.

Even when the words die back,
the stones of our bodies retain a lingering heat.
We read, bones bright with meaning,
cool to a wordless sleep.

Burning Arguments to the Contrary

"I burn for my own lies."
                James Wright

Light leaves your face in leaves.
Weariness settles to the bone.

You wear a mask of iron,
have steeled yourself, wrought
a smile upon your face like a toothache,
lips bloodied by the hammer.

That such distances could be spanned
and emptiness displaced by steel!
Once our days began with the twining
of our bodies, air singed with our welding.

Pig iron rusted to filigree, why can't we
bear the weight of our designing?

Old iron thins to a ragged redness,
is eaten at from both sides,
is dangerous to traverse,
has its own dank smell,
aches of civilization gone sour.

How much harder it is now,
brittle with metal fatigue,
to flee our hollow molds
like sparks leap the firing,
to grind out our gravid beginnings,
to refuse the measure of our bones.

How much harder it is, burning
in the light which leaves your face,
to rectify the pain of my lies.

Hydrangeas in November

Moved by rhythms reaching to their roots,
hydrangeas in November rain sway,
wear crushed corsages of wilted umber.

Dawn is an open window,
screen door slamming,
faded moon packing to leave.

Leaves cartwheel across the sky
like stars, drift like kites,
cords cut by sharp notes.

World settles to earth,
brown to the last shade,
green gone to ground, sleeping.

A Blues Note

To gaze beyond the diamond patterns of the window
is to be unearthed by the ice-hued diamond
of the winter sky, a cloudless, flawless brilliance
uncut by the edge of distance.

                            Lean wind
leans against the panes, sighs ascending patterns,
shifts its weight and whistles. What song,
what melody slips through the window almost
as easily as light?

                       Almost recognized, a rhythm
insignificant yet reminiscent, the singing slips
away like a blue wind sliding over diamond,
unchanged, a momentary moaning of a minor note.

The Winters

To reach the mansion on the ridge,
first find your way among the trees,
their winter-bare windfall of branches
lacing the blue clay of the sky,
untrimmed black shadows entwined
in a wild and winding embrace.

Where the earth is root-heaved,
uneven near the base, trunks curve down,
dormant bodies dreaming soil, roots
veining the marbled grain of bottomland
while on the ridge the red mansion sits,
bricked four-square to the four directions,

to the cardinal geometries of the mind,
plumb with the straight edge of infinity.
Windows reflect upon the blue squares
of the sky, distances within a finite frame.
Stone-cold walls of brick stack
straight into the wind-filled air,

a red-reaching unlike other stone,
a house away from the mess and bother,
from living things which grope and climb
beyond the leaf-bare limbs of trees
to where the cold begins, seeking a place—
this house where the winters live.

Resurrection

"In one creative thought a thousand
forgotten nights of love revive..."
                          Ranier Maria Rilke

I resurrect from the dust of disused years
one night or many, forgotten
and remembered:
                you by twilight,

how you unbutton your blouse
and shrug into nakedness,
how the hollowness within me
is shouldered aside,

how our hands and lips
mouth our slow moaning,
our fingers like tongues
sucked to the knuckle of our desire.

We lay long within that language,
quilting warmth between us.
Oil upon the water was our breathing,
your breasts a bed of poppies.

You sleeping beside me now,
your pale skin like the polish
some stones possess when caressed
by water or willing hands—

I won't shake you from your sleep,
will wait for you to wake, or not.
Kisses will neither change your dream
nor wake you from the lotus of your slumber.

Reflection

> "...and the last turn reveals
> the darker side of what was light before."
> Donald Justice

Glass panes hold off the wind,
but outside the cold continues
late past midnight, late into December,
high into the winter sky
to the darker side of what was light before.

Sky is a gunshot wound,
a powder-burned blue pucker,
space cracked clean of marrow,
bones hollowed to atrophied stone.
The debris of the body is shot and spent,
willing suspension of disbelief a bullet
lodged in the blue veins of a derelict heart.

We drown in the shallows of heaven,
in sight of shoals
where echoes sing of sunlight—
drift in gray flight through broken panes
to the darker side of what was light before.

Three Skies

Where blue sky blurs
the dusky edge of sunset,
three signs, three paths
lead the way through shadow—
three candles and three windows,
three birds in flight,
three embers within the ash.

Night vines like dew upon three flowers;
three seeds lift to leaf after three rains.
When you moisten your lips and smile,
weather blows unasked for,
winds its barefoot way beneath boughs
of bougainvillea, red and purple,
bells storms arbored within your eyes.

Three twilights I walk blind
to the nuance of three shadows cupped
within your hands, shades which melt,
oil the augury of our embraces.
Yes, we must touch one another,
must trace this palmistry of our desire,
this moist, broken beating of our two hearts.

Adoration of Asters

(Butterfly Garden, Jefferson County Park)

Walk with me up this hill, up paths
cut from prairie grasses to where pines
flare green flame, fringe pond.

Sit here with me, just below the crest,
surrounded by flower and wing,
honey and vine, myrrh and frankincense.

Pollen and blossom, these bees know us,
number and nectar, distance and direction,
dance each petal of our dance.

Air is sweet with amber syrup,
boughs of wind resinous with pine.
Like constellations true to the pole star,

stay with me, columbine, butterfly.
Don't leave this very moment. Alight
within this constellation; let us be together.

Honey bees among the asters, let us be together.
Stars and magi dancing, let us be together, bleeding hearts cradled
within the garden of our arms.

Affirmations at the Mouth of the Well

Three dimensions of motion and emotion
are three too many to measure.
The green veins of the asphodel branch
like hands reaching for a more delicate path.
Which way leads to the fruit of your lips,
and in which will shadows cool with twilight?
I wait for weather in which deadwood greens;
sun and shade are children of the same mother.
Let hummingbird and honeysuckle hunger
for the sun, ocarina and owl stitch the night.
Three dimensions of motion and emotion
are three too many to measure.

No danger lies within these words I write.
I wrap myself within the moist fruit of your body,
ripen, orange and black, to a lily of desire,
nude in my need, petals like flaring tusks
luminous in moonlight, marbled by shadow,
meaning a ripe fig sticky with seed.
I cannot sleep for the thought of touching you;
my hands dream in the language of your body.
I want to take your foot, remove the sandal,
find the balance, like a child take that first step.
I want the animal presence of your flesh,
the warmth of your blood in the palm of your hand.

How prudent of me to leave before truth arrives!
I should have stayed, a turtle within the shell,
heeded the voice within the hollow palm of silence.
I who have fallen at the mouth of the well,
moss upon stone, distant sky cold and clear—
sun will not wet me with the waters of its birth
nor will stones offer me the sanctuary of dream.
I need the animal presence of your flesh,
want the ripe fruit of your lips,
hold to what I can throughout the night,
the thought of you nude, meadow in moonlight.
You green the nothingness beyond your skin.

Close your eyes; let us enjoy this night.
Never again will I deny any heart its haven.
Where is the eastern door to your heart?
I am not proud; I need you to be human.
Even when eyes close in sleep, believe me,
currents run deeper than we can swim.
Gill and fin, there are greater waters
than words can give meaning. Current or crossroad,
close your eyes when you reach the center;
stretch your arms, walk barefoot upon this path.
This is what it means to have a human body.
Do not forsake me; embrace these words until they mean.

Bare Ruined Choirs

"Bare ruined choirs where late the sweet birds sang."
                                            William Shakespeare
                                                    Sonnet 73

When you could move no longer, then we moved you—
turned you, held you, your son's eyes averted
from your naked body, his hands placed hip and knee,
fingers wide with an eloquence more familiar with playing fields

than the white sheets of these killing fields—while I, ears blind
to your dying cries, washed from your body effluvia
which seeped from holes, natural and unnatural,
this excretion of bowel and bladder which excoriated flesh,

this drool from cavities and craters and slack-mouthed sores.
You begged me to stop; I told you we were almost finished.
You whimpered and mouthed your pillow; never mind, just forget
the possibility of putrescence within the horror of all these holes.

We all have our limits. A body can only take so much,
must slip from bedside and bed sores to the other side of pain:
must witness this cleansing of the body of the mother,
this absolute certainty there is no other place to be,

nothing other to do than this washing with water
the bare ruined choirs of this ruined body
where late the sweet birds sang, where angels now
avert their eyes, and ache and ache in eloquent silence.

For the Life of Me

The hardest time for me
was when I told you
your mother was going to die.

Mauve walls and stainless steel chairs,
that sterile, hermetic hospital hum—
your silence as you pruned into tears.

Wondering, for the life of me, why
I couldn't keep your mother from dying—
I, who had done everything for ten years,

who could now do nothing but sit,
watching my restless, empty hands
awkward in their awful leisure,

no metaphors at hand, only this image—
father and son holding one another,
holding on by letting go.

Cave Swallow

By the time it was time to say goodbye,
it was too late, too deep within the shadow,
too far within the dark echoing of the cave
where even sound loses its light.

In that dark hollow beyond the last words,
you traveled too far down the fading path,
too far beyond dappled, fortunate years.
Even the most subtle passing of clouds

leaves some footprint in the passing.
Even words unsaid can be heard with perfect clarity.
Like a cliff swallow startling dawn,
you left the cave of your body at sun's rising.

Tell me, foreign to such elegant flight,
how does one leave the cave's crooked shadow,
to break free from the brack of the body,
a wide-eyed swallow sounding the infinite sky?

I Forgive Your Death

I forgive your death
and forgive my living,
forgive the poison of your pain
and the numbering of the days—
forgive that all suns must set,
forgive the dark that lies beneath the sun.

I accept our time between
the apple's first blush
and last puckered wrinkle—
accept the better and the worse,
accept the sickness and the death,
accept forever and ever. Godspeed.

Mother Rose

She reaches through wire squares,
fenced from the flower,
work-calloused hands
bruised blossoms which wrinkle around

the wide-hipped flounce of the rose.
Beyond the weathered bloom of her body,
beyond grey strands of wiry hair,
beyond silent salmon blossoms

leaping scarred stones of a woman's hands
grows a sapling of a woman,
rose vining fence, cleaving to wire,
sunlight shining through rusting squares.

Into the Light

Flecking air
for those who press an ear
to cold stone,

the message is there,
vibration digging down,
voices in the darkness.

Light like a shovel
heavy with meaning,
ore-grimed with color,

we who are blind listen,
air dusted with echoes
ripe with our rites of passage.

Winter Solstice

Clouds like branches heavy with fruit
sag in the sky above the orchard,
raindrops leaning toward their long fall.
Day greys, moss blurs the being of stones,
horizons erode, ravines ruin the sky.

If I could gather enough silence,
I would root myself to this moment,
turn the inedible rind of the seasons
to rhymes ringed in the flesh,
to plum leaves drifting from the branch.

The worm breaches the red flesh of the plum;
leaves burst green from our scars.
The storm works in wet rhythms above me,
air fringed with beads, dark with cloud.
Rain drops from eaves, craters the stillness.

Beyond branches, tendrils of cloud
twine to seams of trellised sunlight,
break through this least of days.
Cloud, rain, this thicket of the sky.
Leaves burst green from our scars.

Winter Pasture

White with prisms
of frosted grass, pastures
glimmer like constellations as the sun rises

a luminous violet
spangled by the iridescent haze
which clouds the frost-covered hills.

The sun yellows as it climbs,
its cool heat a concentric circle
of warmth, a spreading wave of ice-melting fire.

A straw-blond mare
and her yearling foal steam
in the first light, sideways to the sun,

side by side
living each day as it dawns,
their manes and tails like sun-bleached grasses,

their bodies knowing
what we worry with our minds.
Two weeks into winter—this cannot last

we tell ourselves,
just cold enough to be glad
it's not colder, just warm enough to hope.

The pale blue sky
is wiped clean of cirrus clouds
on this southern-sloped pasture of winter,

and into this respite
we fling ourselves like saints into the fire.
If not enlightened, at least we are warm;

if not omniscient,
at least we are smart enough to enjoy
this spring in the winter of our ignorance.

Sonnet 73

by William Shakespeare

That time of year thou mayst in me behold
When yellow leaves, or none, or few, do hang
Upon those boughs which shake against the cold,
Bare ruined choirs, where late the sweet birds sang.
In me thou see'st the twilight of such day
As after sunset fadeth in the west;
Which by and by black night doth take away,
Death's second self, that seals up all in rest.
In me thou see'st the glowing of such fire,
That on the ashes of his youth doth lie,
As the deathbed whereon it must expire,
Consumed with that which it was nourished by.
This thou perceiv'st, which makes thy love more strong,
To love that well which thou must leave ere long.

A Note on the Title

Bare Ruined Choirs

The choir of a church is, traditionally, that section reserved for the singers. Situated between the nave and the sanctuary, the "choir" Shakespeare refers to in "Sonnet 73" is especially significant to the meaning of his poem. The sonnet is about growing older, growing toward that time when we will be "consumed" by the very fires that nourish our life. The final couplet of the sonnet recognizes that one must cherish that which will "leave ere long."

The nave is the main section of a church, and the sanctuary is the most sacred area of the church, wherein the holy of holies lies. Poets are the chorus of God's glory, standing in the choir between the congregation and the transcendent; the aging poet is the "bare ruined choir," the fire of the body spent, night descending upon the body's bones that "shake against the cold."

Through language the poet sings of the cycle of life. Language resides in the choir of our church, articulating the structure of the world yet never able to enter the transcendental reality from which the world manifests. Language stands at the door, waiting for spirit to rise from the transcendent, and then language serves its purpose—sings praises of God to the congregation, sings praises of creation to the Maker. May it be that I have sung my praises with some degree of eloquence.

About the Author

Tom Kepler was born in 1952 in Oroville, California. He earned a B.A. in English, with a specialization in writing poetry, from the University of California, Davis, where he studied with Pulitzer Prize winning poet Karl Shapiro. He later received his K-12 teaching certification from California State University, Chico.

He has previously published in the literary magazines *The Hiram Poetry Review, Wind, California Quarterly, Riverrun,* and *The Galley Sail Review*. His publications also include poetry in the anthology *Leaves by Night, Flowers by Day*.

Currently a faculty member of Maharishi School of the Age of Enlightenment in Fairfield, Iowa, he has been a classroom school teacher and a teacher of the Transcendental Meditation Program for over thirty years. With the help of his beautiful, creative, and dynamic wife, at this time he is seeking to publish his fiction writing.

Book It Forward: a Letter to the Reader

Dear Reader,

Word-of-mouth communication, with the evolution of the internet and social networking, has come to rival the impersonal advertising tools of the mass media.

Print on Demand publishing can now print books one-by-one as they are bought, a more ecologically sound and sustainable practice. This has opened the door for authors to also become publishers, creating a more grassroots, democratic side to the world of books.

It requires your help, though, to "Book It Forward," to tell your friends about a book you've bought that has touched your life.

Send a short email to five friends that *Bare Ruined Choirs* is a book worth buying. Ask them to do the same, to also send five letters.

Be an active reader and Book It Forward.

With sincere thanks,

Tom Kepler

http://sites.google.com/site/tomkeplerwriting/Home/book-it-forward

www.ingramcontent.com/pod-product-compliance
Lightning Source LLC
Chambersburg PA
CBHW032019290426
44109CB00013B/716